THE
BAKER'S BOY
AND THE GREAT FIRE
OF LONDON

First published in 2016 by Wayland
Copyright © Wayland 2016

Wayland
Carmelite House
50 Victoria Embankment
London
EC4Y 0DZ

Wayland Australia
Level 17/207 Kent Street
Sydney NSW 2000

Editor: Katie Woolley
Cover designer: Lisa Peacock
Inside designer: Alyssa Peacock

ISBN: 978 0 7502 9665 6

Printed in China

10 9 8 7 6 5 4 3 2 1

Wayland is a division of
Hachette Children's Group,
an Hachette UK company.
www.hachette.co.uk

THE
BAKER'S BOY
AND GREAT FIRE
THE
OF LONDON

Written by Tom and Tony Bradman

Illustrated by Andy Catling

WAYLAND

CHARACTERS IN THIS STORY...

WILL FARRINER
- a young boy

**THOMAS FARRINER,
WILL'S FATHER**
- a baker

**HANNAH
FARRINER,
WILL'S MOTHER**
- the baker's wife

**PEG - Will's
little sister**

SAMUEL PEPYS
- an important man

ELIZABETH PEPYS
- Samuel's wife

CAPTAIN WHARTON
- leader of The Watch

KING CHARLES II
- the King of England

PROLOGUE

London in 1666 was the biggest, most crowded city in the whole of England. The streets were narrow and the houses were built very closely together. Most were made of wood and had thatched roofs. People used fires to keep warm and to cook their food, and candles to light their homes at night. But some people were careless, too. It would only take one stray spark to start a dangerous blaze.

On 2nd September, that finally happened in a baker's shop on Pudding Lane...

CHAPTER ONE

It was just after midnight when young Will Farriner opened his eyes as he lay in his room above the family baker's shop.

Will could smell smoke – and suddenly he realised what that meant! He leapt from his bed and ran out on to the landing. The smoke was coming from downstairs.

"Wake up, everybody!" Will yelled. "The house is on fire!"

"Will's right," said his father, appearing in his night-shirt. "Something is definitely burning..."

"You must have forgotten to douse the ovens, Thomas!" said his mother.

"This is no time to decide who's to blame," muttered his father. "We have to get out!"

"You're right, I'm sorry," said Will's mother. "Will, you go and fetch your little sister!"

Will dashed to his sister's room and shook her by the shoulder.

"Stop it, Will," Peg mumbled. "It's the middle of the night."

"Come on, Peg," said Will. "Hurry up or we'll be burnt to a crisp!"

Peg smelt the smoke at last. Soon, the family were safely on the street outside where a crowd had gathered.

"The whole house is going up," Will said, holding his little sister close. "We'd better move back!"

"Will we have to buy a new house?" Peg asked.

"What with?" said their father. "All our money is tied up in that shop! We're ruined!"

"Well, at least we're alive," said their mother, pulling the children to her.

Just then, Captain Dick Wharton, leading the men of The Watch, pushed his way through the crowd. The Watch were the city's guardians, the men you called on when you needed help.

"Stand clear, everyone!" said Captain Wharton in a loud voice. "We'll deal with this."

"You'll never save our house now," said Will. Will's mother burst into tears, and Peg did as well. Will's father hugged them both.

"Aye lad, you're right," said Captain Wharton. "But we must stop the fire spreading. We'll have to pull a few houses down. If only we had some gunpowder to get the job done more quickly!"

A murmur went through the crowd when people realised what the captain had said.

"You can't pull down the houses!" someone cried. "They're our homes!"

"I'm sorry," said Captain Wharton. "I'm afraid we don't have much choice."

"It's too late, anyway!" said Will. "Next door's roof is already on fire!"

Within a few minutes, the street was ablaze...

CHAPTER TWO

By the time the sun rose in the morning, the fire had spread a long way. Will and his family had to keep moving as more houses went up in flames.

"Pudding Lane has gone," said Will. "And the next three streets!"

"Hush, Will," his mother whispered. "Your father is upset enough."

"We're doomed!" Will's father groaned. "It is my fault. I should have made sure the ovens were out. The king will probably have me hanged."

Peg burst into tears again, and Will felt utterly useless. Suddenly, he jumped up and ran towards Captain Wharton and The Watch. He didn't want to be useless any more.

"Where are you going, Will?" his mother shouted. "Come back!"

"Just take Peg and Father somewhere safe," Will called out over his shoulder without stopping.

"Hurry, men!" the captain was yelling. "Get some water on that roof before this street goes up, too..."

"I'd like to help, Captain!" said Will.

"Good lad!" said the captain. "Grab a bucket and join the line!"

Will did as he was told. The Watch had tried pulling down some houses in the path of the fire, but that hadn't worked.

The flames were so big they leapt across the gaps. A strong easterly wind was making things worse, too. Small pieces of burning thatch and wood whirled through the air like tiny stars, and more flames leapt up wherever they landed.

The men of The Watch were also collecting water from horse troughs and wells on street corners, filling buckets and forming lines to pass them along. But even when they set up a line that stretched all the way to London's great river, the Thames, the flames simply burned on.

The fire consumed another street, and another. Everything in its path was destroyed – houses, taverns, hospitals and churches. As Captain Wharton, his men and Will retreated, they heard a loud cracking noise.

"Look out!" yelled Captain Wharton. He pulled Will to one side just as the building's roof fell down on where they had been standing moments before. The flames leapt into yet another street, and Will felt a chill run down his spine. The fire was like a living creature.

"We're not getting anywhere, Captain," said Will. "What else can we do?"

"We need more men," said the captain. "I must send someone to the palace to ask the king."

"I'll be happy to go for you, Captain!" said Will.

The captain nodded then turned back to the fight the fire. Will ran off, heading down the street towards the palace as fast as he could go. Behind him, the flames lit up the night sky.

CHAPTER THREE

It was quiet in the west of the city. A few people were pointing to the smoke rising in the east, but most were getting on with their business.

Will followed the crowd entering through the gates of the king's palace. As he crossed the courtyard and went through another door, a guard stopped him.

"Where do you think you're going?" said the guard. "Scruffs like you can't be in the palace!"

"You must let me in!" he said, feeling desperate. "I have to talk to the king about the fire!"

"What fire? You're just spinning me a line so you can get in," said the guard. "Be off with you! The king has no time for such tall tales."

"But I'm not telling a tale, I swear!" said Will.

"That's enough!" said the guard. He grabbed Will and dragged him back towards the door.

"Let go of the boy at once," said an important-looking man. "He's telling the truth. I've seen the fire myself."

"Er… of course, Mr Pepys," said the guard.

"You'd better come with me, lad," Mr Pepys said. "I'm on my way to tell the king about the fire."

So, this was the famous Mr Samuel Pepys who worked for the king, thought Will. As Will and Mr Pepys hurried through the grand rooms, all the guards saluted and the finely-dressed courtiers nodded. Will noticed that Mr Pepys's clothes were just as sooty and singed as his own!

At last, they came to the king's audience chamber. The king was sitting on his throne, surrounded by more courtiers.

"Ah, Pepys!" the king frowned. "Why are you in such an awful mess?"

Mr Pepys bowed. "I am sorry, Your Majesty," he said. "I have come here straight from the east of the city where a fire has broken out."

"There are always fires in London," said the king with a shrug. "That is what Captain Wharton and The Watch are for."

"Perhaps not this time," said Pepys. "The fire is moving too quickly!"

"Calm down, Pepys!" said the king. "And who is this young man?"

"Will Farriner, Your Majesty," said Will, and he bowed. "Mr Pepys is right. Captain Wharton says he needs more men to fight the fire."

"Does he now?" said the king. "And where have I heard your name before?"

"My father, Thomas Farriner, makes the best pastries in London, Your Majesty," Will said.

"So he does!" said the king. "It seems there is no time to lose. Summon the army, Pepys!"

Moments later, Will was hurrying back towards the fire with Mr Pepys and some soldiers. He only hoped they wouldn't be too late...

CHAPTER FOUR

Back at the fire, things were going very badly.
By the time Will arrived with Mr Pepys and the
soldiers from the palace, even more streets were
burning. Captain Wharton and his men were
in the thick of it, and lots of Londoners were
helping, too. But the fire was still leaping from
house to house.

"We've brought help, Captain!" said Will.

"Well done, lad!" said the captain. "We need it now more than ever!"

The captain quickly got the soldiers organised, some in lines with buckets, the rest pulling down thatched roofs before they caught fire. Arguments broke out as the people who lived in the houses tried to stop them. Others were dragging their furniture out and were getting in the firefighters' way.

There was thick, choking smoke everywhere, and everyone was coughing. It was hot, too, the air scorching Will's throat with each breath. His shoulders ached but he kept going, grabbing the buckets of water from the person behind him and passing them on to Mr Pepys. Still, the fire raged on…

"Retreat!" the captain called out after a while. "We've lost this street, too!"

Just then, more soldiers arrived, led by the king himself. "Sorry I have been a while," he said. "I have been trying to round up as many men as possible."

"It's good of you to come at all, Your Majesty!" said the captain.

"Nonsense!" said the king. "Everyone must join in the fight!"

But before long another building collapsed in a shower of sparks and smoke.

Will and Mr Pepys found themselves separated from everyone else.

"I give up," said Mr Pepys in despair. "London is finished!"

"Then I must go to my family before it's too late," said Will.

He turned to run off, but Mr Pepys held him back. "It's too dangerous, Will. You'll never find them in this chaos! You'd better come with me."

They ran through streets full of panicking people and finally came to Mr Pepys's house. Mr Pepys's wife Elizabeth was relieved to see him.

"Samuel, I've been so worried about you!" she said, hugging him tight. "But you look terrible! Where have you been? And who is this boy?"

"His name is Will," said Mr Pepys. "No time to talk – we have to get out of here, and take our valuables. Except the cheese. We'll bury that."

"You're going to bury some cheese?" said Will. "Are you quite all right, sir?"

"It's a piece of Italian cheese, and it's worth a great deal of money," said Mr Pepys. "I'd better bury my official papers, too. Could you help me, Will?"

The papers were in a large wooden chest. Will took one end and Mr Pepys the other. But they were tired and dropped it, spilling the papers on the floor. Will started picking them up, then noticed something on one of the pages.

"Captain Wharton told me he could stop the fire quickly if he had enough gunpowder," Will said. "And according to this there's a lot in the Tower of London."

"Will, you're a genius!" said Mr Pepys, grinning. "Quick, there's no time to lose! Don't stay here, Elizabeth — you must go somewhere safe."

Soon, Will and Mr Pepys were running, back towards the flames this time.

CHAPTER FiVE

It took Will and Mr Pepys ages to find Captain Wharton and the king. The fire was out of control, and Will could see that a large part of the city was ablaze. He and Mr Pepys kept finding their way blocked, either by the flames or the crowds. Will had almost given up hope, but then he glimpsed the pair through the smoke.

"Your Majesty! Captain Wharton!" Will yelled. He skidded to a halt in front of them and started gabbling breathlessly. "I know what to do... Mr Pepys's cheese... his papers falling out... it's all in the Tower of London!"

"Whoa, slow down!" said the king. "You'll have to tell us again! And start at the beginning."

Will took a deep breath and did just that, but more slowly this time. When he had finished, the king turned to Captain Wharton. "Is the boy right, Captain?"

"Yes, Your Majesty," said the captain. "We just
have to blow up some houses in the right places."

"Is there enough gunpowder to do the job and

stop the fire spreading, Pepys?" asked the king.

"Oh yes, Your Majesty," said Mr Pepys. "My records show there is enough gunpowder in the Tower to blow up half of London."

Well, carry on," said the king. "It sounds like an excellent idea!"

Mr Pepys gave the order and some of the king's soldiers hurried off to the Tower of London. There, they loaded barrels of gunpowder on to wagons and brought them back to the captain. He had decided where they should go and the soldiers worked quickly, stacking them and laying a gunpowder fuse.

At last everything was ready – and then the king turned to Will.

"I think it's only right that you should do the honours, young man," said the king.

"What, me?" said Will, and the king nodded.

Will gulped as the captain gave him a lit match. He walked over and held it to the nearest end of

the fuse. The gunpowder took a while to catch – then it sparked and fizzed, and a tiny flame raced towards the stack of barrels.

"I think we should probably all take cover," said the captain. Just then, there was a big BANG! A whole street of houses was blown up, leaving a huge gap that the flames couldn't cross.

"It worked!" yelled the captain. "The fire has finally been stopped!"

"Well done, young man," said the king, as everybody cheered. "You deserve a reward for what you have done today – you can have anything you want!"

Suddenly, Will heard somebody calling his name. He looked round and saw his family pushing through the crowd. The four of them hugged each other.

"Are you all right, Will?" said his mother.

"I'm fine," said Will, grinning. "Mr Pepys has been looking after me."

"Thank you, sir," said Will's father.

"Oh, think nothing of it," said Mr Pepys. "Your son is a hero now. He has saved London!"

"He most certainly is," said the king. "You should be proud of him."

Will's parents hadn't noticed the king till then.

Now Will's mother froze in utter shock, and his father fell to his knees. "I'm so sorry, Your Majesty!" he wailed. "I didn't mean to start the fire! It was an accident, I swear it was!"

"So you're the one to blame!" said the king. "Arrest him, Captain!"

"Wait a moment!" yelled Will. "You said I could have a reward. I want you to pardon my father... and give him enough money to start a new bakery."

"Well, your father does make exceedingly good cakes..." said the king, rubbing his chin thoughtfully. "Fine, it's a deal. But there is one condition, Mr Farriner."

"Yes, Your Majesty?' said Will's father.

"Do try to be a little more careful in future," said the king.

"Don't worry,' Your Majesty," said Will. "We'll make sure of that!"

And everybody laughed, Will loudest of all.

GLOSSARY

detachment
a group of
soldiers

douse
to put
something out

fuse
material
along which a
flame moves

thatched
a roof that is
covered with
straw

The Watch
London's
combined police
and fire brigade
in the 17th
century

Library of Congress Cataloging-in-Publication Data Available

ISBN 978-1-250-02775-7 (hardcover)
1 3 5 7 9 10 8 6 4 2

ISBN 978-1-250-02776-4 (paperback)
1 3 5 7 9 10 8 6 4 2

Book design by Patrick Collins/Véronique Lefèvre Sweet

Square Fish logo designed by Filomena Tuosto

Originally published in similar form as *Leopard & Silkie*
by Christy Ottaviano Books, an imprint of Henry Holt and Company, 2012.
First My READERS Edition: 2013

myreadersonline.com
mackids.com

This is a Level 2 book

Lexile 570L

 **Dear Par**

In an easy-reader form
who are learning to read.
fascinating facts to children

My Readers are available in th

1 **Level One** is for the
repetitive language and word

2 **Level Two** is for more advan
need support saying and understan
Stories are longer with word clues in the

3 **Level Three** is for independent, fluent rea
enjoy working out occasional unfamiliar words
stories are longer and divided into chapters.

Encourage children to select books based on interests, not reading le
Read aloud with children, showing them how to use the illustrations fo
clues. With adult guidance and rereading, children will eventually read the
desired book on their own.

Here are some ways you might want to use this book with children:

- Talk about the title and the cover illustrations. Encourage
  the child to use these to predict what the story is about.
- Discuss the interior illustrations and try to piece together a
  story based on the pictures. Does the child want to change
  or adjust his first prediction?
- After children reread a story, suggest they retell or act out
  a favorite part.

My Readers will not only help children become readers, they will serve as
an introduction to some of the finest classic children's books available today.

—LAURA ROBB
Educator and Reading Consultant

For activities and reading tips, visit myreadersonline.com.

Seal Pup Rescue

Brenda Peterson

photographs by **Robin Lindsey**

SQUARE
FISH

Macmillan Children's Publishing Group
New York

Leopard is born at sunrise

on a summer day.

He is a golden, spotted seal pup.

Leopard is shorter

than a skateboard

and weighs a little more

than a bowling ball.

Leopard's white and wavy fur

looks dark when it's wet.

Leopard nuzzles

with his mother.

Then he drinks a bellyful

of rich milk.

His mother learns

her pup's scent and sounds

so she can find him

when they are apart.

Leopard explores the beach.
He uses his foreflippers
to hop and slide
along the sand.

Leopard is only one hour old,

but it's time

for his first swimming lesson.

"Maaaaa!" he calls.

Leopard plays in shallow rock pools.

When he gets tired,

he catches a ride

on his mother's back.

Leopard naps in a secret cove
while his mother fishes nearby.
Is Leopard safe?

Yes, he is.

Miles is watching.

Miles is a Seal Sitter.

Seal Sitters help protect seal pups.

Miles knows it's natural

for pups like Leopard to nap onshore.

The sea is cold,

so pups warm up on the beach.

13

The next day,

Leopard is alone onshore,

waiting for his mother.

The beach is filled with people.

They look like giants to Leopard.

They come too close

and talk too loud.

"Is the seal dead?" children ask.

"Where is the mother?"

Leopard is very scared.

He has never seen people before.

Will they hurt him?

Will they steal him from the beach?

16

Leopard shivers

and covers his face to hide.

"Please, stand back!" says Miles.

"This pup is just resting.

The mother may be watching us

from the water."

Miles asks people

to put their dogs on leashes.

Then Miles puts up

yellow tape around Leopard.

It reads "Protected Marine Mammal."

This keeps people away

from Leopard.

They can watch him

with their binoculars.

Leopard rolls on his back and yawns.

He even falls asleep.

Soon Miles has another idea.

He helps build a large raft

of plywood and foam.

A floating island!

Leopard can rest there

when the beach gets crowded.

Other Seal Sitters

help watch over Leopard

until the raft is finished.

Miles and other Seal Sitters

row out with the raft

into the cold waves.

He ties the raft to a buoy

just offshore.

But Leopard does not leave the beach.

Is he too scared to swim

out to the raft by himself?

Miles waits
and worries.

Suddenly, a head appears

in the waves.

"Maaaaa!" Leopard cries,

and he flop-hops

from the beach into the surf.

Then Leopard and his mother

leap up onto the raft!

The seals wave and flap their flippers.

Leopard and his mother

swim together.

Leopard learns how to catch fish.

Then they relax with friends.

Now Leopard has

a safe place to sleep

while his mother is away.

Leopard sleeps and dreams,

and like good friends,

the Seal Sitters

watch over him.

Author's Note

Seals spend half their lives on the shores. Mothers usually give birth on land. There, they nurse and rest and warm up. But beaches are busy. That's why Seal Sitters watch over marine mammals. If you are near a coast that has seals, you can, too. If not, you can still help keep beaches clean by picking up trash and plastics like balloons.

If you see any seal pups on the beach, call your NOAA Marine Mammal Stranding Network. Keep dogs on leashes. Stay a safe distance away. Watch through your binoculars.

Be a good neighbor and share the land with seals like Leopard. It's fun. And you can save a life!

For more information, go to: www.leopardandsilkie.com.